D1519572

Good Enough

The Wild Woman's Guide to Finding Love
without Losing Her Soul

Stacey J. Warner

Copyright

Table of Contents

Introduction

Clocks slay time...time is dead as long as it is being clicked off by little wheels; only when the clock stops does time come to life.

— William Faulkner

You are a bold, dynamic, modern woman who spent her 20's and/or 30's creating a successful career or being a badass entrepreneur, thinking love would surely find its way to you.

Maybe you've thought things like:

- "When I make partner, then I'll meet him."
- "Med school is where I'll find him."
- "After I've published my first book and I'm out on tour…"
- "When I've opened my yoga studio…"
- "When I land my first paid acting gig…"

And now your biological clock is ticking loudly, but you still don't want to settle. You know that true love trumps baby, and doing it alone isn't in your future. You've probably gone over all your options again and again: freeze your eggs, adopt later in life, settle for a man who would be a great dad, a friend you've made a pact with, IVF, sperm donor … the list goes on.

You might have even beaten yourself up a bit for focusing so hard on your career, thinking you were doing the right thing; that your time would come as you stood, holding the wedding bouquet over and over again, watching your friends say 'I do;' wondering, *when will it be my turn?*

Now you are ready to focus on dating. You are ready for a relationship. It's time, but it seems like something isn't working every time you go on a date. It just never feels right, and you wonder if he can actually hear the relentless ticking of your biological clock through your words or actions. Perhaps you've had the thought, *true love is just not for me. I'm not the kind of woman that men fall in love with.*

I'm here to tell you that you are worthy of love and what is keeping you from finding it might not be what you think it is. Love is about intimacy, about being vulnerable and letting down your guard. You are successful because you have it all handled — you are good at what you do; you are tough; you are organized; basically, you are a bad ass. You are a survivor. But underneath of all the strength, what are you? Love asks us to put aside everything that has given us stability and to open yourself up to the mystery of life, where things don't feel quite so controlled.

Several years ago, my life coach said to me, "I would never date you. You are too tough," in front of everyone in the group. I held back tears, which is kind of funny, since *not crying* supported his statement. Still, I was not going to let him see me cry. It was incredibly difficult to hear this from a man I admired and had put my trust into, and so the words stuck with me. Was it right for him to say this? Probably not, but from that day forward I committed myself to dismantling my persona of 'tough.'

Underneath this tough exterior was a broken little girl that wanted to be saved. Is this true for you? Or, how about something like this?

I was first introduced to *The Return of the Native* by Thomas Hardy in high school. Upon first opening the pages, I was also introduced to my favorite heroine, Eustacia Vye. Eustacia, an exotic, dark haired, queenly beauty, was born and raised on Egdon Heath, a depressing environment that she couldn't wait to escape from, much like my own childhood home. In the story, she day dreams about a man that would swoop her up, love her, and save her by taking her off the heath.

After much romantic intrigue, Eustacia falls for Clym Yeobright, a handsome, local hero who returns to the heath and woos her by promising to take her away. But he never does. He decides to stay on the heath, goes blind by studying to become a teacher, and breaks Eustacia's heart in the process. He is the golden boy that everyone expected so much from, doomed to a tragic ending.

As the reality of Eustacia's circumstance hits her, she realizes that her marriage has become an additional chain to her familiar prison of the heath. What she feared the most has somehow come to fruition. She tries to find peace with it until she can take it no longer and takes her fate into her own hands, attempting escaping with another man, only to commit suicide before following through.

Super dark and tragic, right? The complexity of these characters speaks to my soul. At the time of the novel's publication, the possibilities for women were so limited that being saved by a man was perhaps seen as a viable option, as was the trope of holding out for your true love to whisk you away from your state of distress. I, too, wanted to escape my childhood surroundings, wanted true love to save me, and discovered that every handsome man I saw as a hero was actually a tragic figure. In turn, I viewed marriage as a prison. The thought of marrying the wrong man or not having my freedom scared me to death, so I kept myself a courtesan: smart, witty, great conversationalist, aloof, personifying a person I thought was free. But this, too, became a sort of prison.

I wish I had a really cool fix-all process, series, keys, or steps to lead you to the love of your life to start a family, but the truth is that your life and your soul are beautifully complex, you are a labyrinth, and all I can do is guide you with the wisdom I have gained and the gifts I have received from the wisdom. The rest is up to you.

Change is incredibly difficult. It is why most people do not change but rather step blindly into their fate, without the will to step onto a new path. In this book, we will uncover what keeps you from finding love. It's not about the amount of men in your social circle, the city you are in, or your ability to play the 'game' well. It's far more romantic than that.

You are a beautiful heroine. Maybe you have your own tragic story. Maybe you've survived more than you thought you could. Maybe you feel that, because of this, you've lost your chance for love and a family. Whatever the story is you've created, I can assure you it isn't true.

For 47 years, I was lost in my own story, until I chose to dig deep into my own subconscious, opening up the deeper channels of my heart, looking into the dark corners where I had been afraid to look. I realized that by doing this, I was actually loving myself and no longer needed to be saved from that inner, fearful place. I became a woman, the heroine of my own story.

I want this for you, and I want this for you sooner than later because I know you have children on your mind. So pull up a chair, pour a glass of wine, or make a cup of tea and get cozy. I'm thrilled to be on this journey with you. I will open my heart to you. Keep your heart open and we will go far, creating a new story full of love, intrigue, romance, and dreams coming true, just for you.

Chapter 1: You Are Your Greatest Love Affair

It is not in the stars to hold our destiny but in ourselves.

— *William Shakespeare*

I sat on the toilet and peed, tapping my feet against the cold tile floor. I had hoped that somehow this might change my fate, flushing the sperm away before it reached my fertile egg. I knew it was crazy. I'd never heard of anyone not getting pregnant because they peed after a "slip," but it was the first thing that came to mind. So, there I was, peeing.

It wasn't that I didn't want to have a baby. In fact, at thirty-two, I just couldn't take watching another one of my friends walk down the aisle and, a year later, announce that she was pregnant. It was too depressing. So, I planned a spur-of-the moment move to Bali, where I planned to work as a yoga teacher, write on the side, and avoid thinking about my lack of a relationship and lack of child. If I'm being really honest with myself, it was an *escape*. I was desperate, and Bali in February was the answer. Or so I thought.

I crawled back into bed, next to the possible baby-daddy.

"I just got pregnant," I whispered, not really wanting him to hear, but needing to say it out loud. He rolled away from me, more interested in sleep. I lay next to him, counting out the months to when the baby would be due: February.

This guy was not my boyfriend. He had been previously, but on this night he was just a booty-call. We had dated for nine months and had been separated for the same amount of time. After the break-up, I became a yoga teacher and spent my life in meditation. Maybe *too* much meditation, since I often felt like I was floating three inches off the ground. I then had the brilliant idea that having sex would help me "come down to earth.". It so happened that my ex was available and seemed to be doing a bit of work on himself as well.

Our relationship had been like a Movie of the Week, with me a co-dependent love addict, him just an addict, and the two of us entangled until our final conflict. Our relationship came to a head on, of all days, 9/11. That morning, after the first tower crashed to the ground, I had driven zombie-like to work. Once there, and after watching the second tower collapse, I called him crying.

He asked, "What are you crying about?" as if he didn't know that that thousands of people were dying. Of course, he did know, and he spent the rest of the day in a bar, playing pool and drinking, while I communed with girlfriends, devouring the news and pizza. Later that night, he passed out on my couch. It was then that I knew it was over.

Then, nine months later and after one lapse of judgement, here we were in bed, with me wondering how I (or we) would manage to raise this baby —if the pregnancy turned out to be true.

Two weeks later, we sat at Coffee Bean and Tea Leaf, waiting for my doctor's appointment. We had continued to see each other, but we weren't gushing and giddy like two people falling back in love. We were fairly certain this wasn't going to work and were just waiting to see if I was pregnant.

"If you don't want to be a part of this, you can walk away," I told him. "I won't come looking for you, " I said waving his cigarette smoke out of my face.

But he had been reared by a single mother and had experienced that hardship first-hand, so his sense of guilt would have him going nowhere. At the doctor's office, my pregnancy test came back negative. Ryan glowed when I told him, but I was fairly certain I could still feel the cells dividing in my uterus. His relief would be temporary.

We went to see *Minority Report* in the theater, and it was there that I knew for certain that I was pregnant. During the most intense scenes of the movie, I could feel this tiny being's emotions vibrating through me. I touched my stomach and smiled, in awe of what was happening —also scared.

After the movie, we got in the car and began having a huge argument in his truck over him smoking around me. In that moment, I thought it would be a relief if I wasn't pregnant; a relief to never have to see this guy again.

When we got home, I turned on my cell phone; and there was a message. It was my doctor. I was pregnant. Apparently, the test turned positive after we left his office. Ryan tried to put his arms around me in an embrace, but I got up and paced, tears of joy and fear competing within me. I finally collapsed on the bed, crying.

"I'm tiny. I'm tiny," I wept. "I'm so little in this bigness of creating life. I feel so small."

Then Ryan cried. Whether they were tears of joy or pain, I'll never know. What I do know is that we were on an unexpected journey together, whether we liked it or not. Who knew where it would lead? For me, it wasn't Bali in February. It was a baby.

Even if your eggs are screaming, I do not suggest getting accidentally pregnant with an ex. My baby-daddy has been my greatest lesson, but it's also been an incredibly difficult journey raising a child with him. It meant that I missed out on an opportunity to relax during my pregnancy. I never got to share the experience with a friend, nor did I really get to share it with Ryan. After I found out I was pregnant, my baby-daddy and I moved in together, but it only lasted two months. He drank too much and was too disrespectful, so I made the second biggest move of my life and moved out. I was completely exhausted, lonely, and scared. I felt like a victim in my own life.

Flash forward to 2007 — I had made it through the first few years of motherhood. I was busy raising my 4-year-old and learning important life lessons about community, asking for help, and discovering how to co-parent with a toxic human being. I also started getting another itch to have a baby and I knew time was running out. I was 37. I ran the numbers again like I did when I was 32. If I went the traditional route, I was probably going to be about 40 before I'd be married, and that's if I found a man right away.

This was the year I started a blog called SingleMILF. My intent was to write about my experience dating as a single mother. I joined a bunch of online dating sites, which were not as popular or accepted as they are today. To put it in perspective, iPhones had just been announced so all on-line dating was literally done sitting at your computer.

About two weeks after getting on dating sites and getting my blog up, I met a man. It was love at first sight. We dated, got engaged, planned a wedding, rescheduled the wedding, and cancelled the rescheduled wedding in the course of three months. We had talked about having a child together, and it felt so right that we rushed things. Instead of my blog being about care-free, love-filled dating, it was about the intense and highly codependent relationship I had with this man.

Obviously, I don't do anything traditionally. I still don't. I've always been chasing love, free diving with my heart.

In retrospect, even acknowledging how foolish I was and how I created so much of my own suffering, I wouldn't change it for the world. But I also wouldn't want to repeat the lessons, and that's the true magic of it all. There is nothing to regret except not taking risks and getting out there. You are reading this book because you truly desire a relationship and your biological clock is ticking. I hear you. I've been there, a few times. I can help you find it for yourself and avoid some of the pitfalls along the way. But remember, there is much to learn, even in the pitfalls. It is better to be doing something and making mistakes than to be doing nothing. If you are doing nothing, then nothing can happen.

I discovered why relationship remained elusive to me, and this is the gift I will give you. If you are willing to open up and see magic, magic appears. We can only control so much and then we have to believe and trust in something bigger than ourselves.

Throughout the moments of feeling like there was no hope, I forged forward, knowing that just around the corner there could be a chance meeting, but I had to keep putting one foot in front of the other and find the romance in the trenches.

Remember, you are your greatest love affair. Let the romance begin.

Chapter 2: It's Never Too Late

What matters is precisely this; the unspoken at the edge of the spoken.

— Virginia Woolf

I stared at the grapefruit, mouthwatering but not in a good way. My gag reflex was on high alert. I hated grapefruit, but that didn't matter. "I'll pick us grapefruit for breakfast," he'd said the night before, looking out the window at his grapefruit tree. And with just those six words, I imagined us staring into each other's eyes over shared grapefruit and finally falling in love. I'd do anything to make this a reality, including forcing grapefruit down my throat.

'He,' was Ken, a 43-year-old, single dad divorcee who I'd met a year earlier on chemistry.com. Ken had warned me on our first phone call that I should run for the hills. All I heard was *catch me if you can.* Our first date consisted of a Ferris wheel ride on the Santa Monica Pier, a drink, and lots of making out. As far as I was concerned, I was done, and he was *the one.* Our chemistry was instant and powerful. With his hands on my hips, pressing me against him, I was on fire and I wanted to burn more, to be devoured and released from what had become my life — raising my son alone, a corporate job, and dealing with my baby-daddy. I was on automatic pilot on a dullard's flight. Ken was adventure.

We dated, cooked, and went to concerts. We meditated on the beach and did yoga. We hung out with Cole, my 5 year old son, and went to parties with my friends. We connected and disconnected; I never felt he was "all in," and I struggled with his distance. He knew I was hooked and kept the leverage by monitoring my doses. My friends didn't like him, and Cole was cool towards him. I was in deep, but he treaded water —preferring the surface while I dove down.

After six months of nearly drowning, I stopped communicating with him and suffered in silence, missing the smell of his Calvin Klein cologne, his touch, and the anticipation of seeing him. I met a nice guy, an all-in guy, and started dating him. Months passed, and I was able to ignore Ken's one or two texts until he emailed me a picture of his son. My stomach sank.

During our time apart, Ken had moved from Long Beach back to Lake Elsinore and was working as a skydiving instructor and photographer again. He had also been allowed to see his son. But I wasn't sure that was the only preson he was seeing. He also said his ex-wife was living with her mother. She'd lost her house and her car. She sounded desperate. And, in a way, so was he. And so was I.

Ken landed on my doorstep less than a week later. I opened the door and wrapped my arms around him, held his face in my hands and breathed him in again.

I continued to pick at my grapefruit while I watched Ken scarf his down. There was no gazing into each other's eyes. We weren't falling in love. In fact, the air was chilly.

He sprang to his feet to get ready for his day of skydiving. I looked around his sparsely furnished, doublewide mobile home. Did I really want this life? A mobile home in an abandoned suburban area? I glanced around for signs that other women had been there. The sheer purple curtains were suspect.

I buried my grapefruit in the trash like I used to do as a child, hiding food I hated from my father. Ken walked back into the kitchen half dressed. *Damn he was hot,* I thought as he pulled the coffee pod from the espresso machine to make a second cup.

"Oh, I'd love one," I said.

Ken slammed the pod down, "Can I get some help here?"

I shot up like a little girl getting yelled at by her father.

"Maybe I can do the eggs," I asked paralyzed by fear.

"No, just sit down," he barked at me. I withdrew and sat again.

A few minutes later, I was standing by my car, hugging him good-bye with a feeling I'd never see him again. On the drive home, it became clear that I was recreating my childhood home of emotional abuse. I wanted none of it, but my feelings for Ken did not go away. I spent the next two weeks bouncing between heart and head.

It went from, *"…if I hadn't lost myself, he'd have loved me…,"* to, *"He's a jerk, you don't want him anyway…,"* and *" you're going to live in the IE (Inland Empire), really?"* These thoughts went on and on until finally, my heart won and I called him.

"I love you and I think we have a future together," I said, simply and clearly.

"I love spending time with you," he said.

I hung up the phone, freshly wounded. Again.

It was time to cut the ties. But one night, a couple of weeks later, after drinking some wine, I sent a flirty text.

"I'm dating my ex-wife again...thought I should tell you," he replied the next day. "After all, you've been a great teacher and an influence on myself."

I couldn't breathe.

"Be well, good luck." I replied. "Just remember a leopard doesn't change its spots. This woman kept you from your son for vengeance. Now you are in bed with her. It's not love. It is ego in its truest form... Give my love to your son, who is being used as a pawn."

"LOL!..." he replied.

But then I softened: *What if they really did think they were back in love?*

I backed off and wrote: "I do pray you both heal through your love for one another..."

"Whatever Stacey...see you," were his last words to me.

Summer turned to fall, Christmas came and went, and I never heard from him. I assumed he was living happily ever after, but I never gave up hope that he would call and tell me he loved me.

Around the first of February, I decided I was brave enough to go on his Facebook page and possibly see the happy photos of his new life. Sitting at work, with my insides churning, I went to his page. I clicked on the first picture I saw of him. The text beneath read, "I will miss this smile."

I continued to scroll down. What was I looking at? It was like witnessing a horrible accident —a bumper here, a mirror there, the burn of tire tracks over there. I couldn't piece together what I was reading. Ken was dead? It couldn't be true. I collapsed under my desk, gasping for air.

I spent the rest of the afternoon shattered, slowly piecing some of the information together. I emailed his mother.

She replied and told me that Ken had died on Sunday, July 18, 2010. (Just five weeks after our last text). It was his fifth jump of the day. He had been using a new rig (the one we went to look at the night we were together) and hit an air pocket about 200 feet up, causing the chute to collapse with no time to recover. He had two broken legs, a broken pelvis, ruptured spleen and massive internal bleeding. He died five hours later on the operating table.

It's been eight years since Ken's death. I have mourned him on multiple levels throughout the years. It's been quite the journey — one full of mystical coincidences. Aside from Ken's passing, telling this story again in such detail makes me cringe. It's so obvious I was lost, horribly lost.

I wish I could have taken my younger self out for coffee to tell her a few things. First I would tell her to heed a man's words, if he say's 'run for the hills,' do it. Know what you want, don't settle for less, speak your truth, and if you don't like grapefruit, say it. Stay out of fantasy, it's your worse enemy. And no drunk texting!

So how did I go from the emotional level of a little girl, eating much-hated grapefruit, to a strong woman, not desperately seeking relationship?

By learning that my relationship with myself is the most important relationship. If I do something that isn't caring for me, showing up for me, the rest doesn't matter. I learned to have my own back and trust my gut.

In other words, yes, I'm talking about self-love. But I also hate that term. And what does 'self love' really mean? Sounds like a bunch of BS. I sought self love for most of my adult life. It was the proverbial carrot always dangling ahead of me, illusive. I truly believed that once I loved myself (whatever that meant) the gates of heaven would open up, but it wasn't like that. It was more like, *shit, this is who I am and this is how I've been showing up (or not showing up) for myself?*

In real terms, how does one realize self love? If we take a look at the grapefruit story, where do you think I stopped showing up for myself? Maybe when I ate the grapefruit? Nope, it was actually the year before, when I first met Ken and he started playing games with me. I thought I was cool, twisting myself up into pretzels trying to make it work for me, telling myself that I just wanted sex like he did, that I didn't need a full on commitment, that crumbs were better than the whole loaf, etc.

The truth was that I thought I was completely in love with Ken and wanted to build a life with him, maybe have a baby with him, but he wasn't available. I allowed myself to be tortured for a year, believing he was the only man in the world that could offer me great sex and adventure. If I had loved myself, I would have seen all the red flags and moved on a little faster.

Let's flash forward 7 years — I'd been dating a guy for about six weeks. I had a feeling he was not going to be *the one*, but I liked him. He seemed like an alright guy. One evening, we made plans for dinner. Around lunch the day of our date, he found himself in my neighborhood, so I invited him over. Yes, it was for a nooner and once we were 'done,' he left quickly. There was something about his good-bye that had my gut twist in knots.

About an hour later, he texted me that he needed to cancel dinner plans. What? My pulse raced. I texted him that it was totally uncool to come over, have sex, and then cancel dinner plans. 'I knew I was going to receive a text like this,' he texted back.

I thought to myself, *then why would he even cancel plans? This isn't the guy for me.* I broke up with him. You can only imagine his shock. I'm sure he'd gotten use to women sticking around, even with this sort of behavior. He was in control, getting sex for as long as he wanted before moving on. This wasn't going to work for me. I had gotten to the point where I knew what I wanted and wasn't going to mess around with someone. I showed up for myself. I showed more love for my *self* than desperately trying to make it work with this guy.

Again, you are probably asking how did you go from a woman eating grapefruit, which you hate, to a woman who could easily say good-bye to a man that just canceled a dinner date? First, let me explain, that it wasn't the canceled dinner date that was the main problem, everyone makes mistakes, changes plans, etc. What made me break up with him was his response to me. I have very little experience in committed relationships, but the one thing I do know is that I need a partner who is willing to discuss and show interest in my point of view, especially when it differs from theirs. This is the foundation of a healthy relationship. This guy showed no ability or interest in communication.

This book is a divine romance between, you, your Self, me, and your future partner, who, by the way, can't wait to meet you. Remember you are special, but you are not so special that you are going to be the unlucky one out of all your girlfriends to die alone without children.

The first step to all great romance is to date.

Open All The Doors and Windows, Sage the Place

The key to finding love is to open yourself up. To find love, you must date. There is no other way around it. As Dr. Pat Allen, one of my favorite dating gurus, calls it, *duty dating*. The man of your dreams is not going to just knock on your door. It's a lovely fantasy, but it's not going to happen. If you have a strong negative opinion about online dating, dating services, dating, or men in general, this could be why you are single. But don't worry, I got you. We'll go deeper into all of this and rediscover your true essence, that little girl inside you that once believed in true love. She's there, just a little worn out. I'll show you how to make dating fun, easy and an adventure. Every date is an opportunity to fall more in love with yourself.

Time to Get Real!

Fantasy is your worst enemy while dating or in relationship. The sort of relationship you truly want cannot be founded in fantasy. It will leave you unhappy. Imagine building a house on sand — that's what fantasy is to a relationship and/or dating. I know this because fantasy was my drug of choice. Usually, when I first start working with clients, they would often think their 'meh' date will turn into prince charming. Remember, Cinderella was the one who changed, it wasn't the prince. The prince was always the prince. Its time break the cycle of fantasy and denial. The mana of life is in the trenches —reality. One of my clients just sent me the following quote from Terry Real, "In order to be intimate you have to bring yourself up from shame and down from grandiosity. This is an essential skill to master in relationships." Magic is always happening. Are you open to it? It's hard to experience when you are in fantasy or denial.

Ready to Find Your Lotus Flower?

And I'm not talking about your vagina ... or am I? Ha! Often, when I first start working with a client, I tell her that to date successfully, she needs to imagine herself as a queenly woman lounging on a lotus flower, ready to receive. Feminine energy is not a woman seeking out a man, focused, determined, almost frightening in a predatory stance. A woman receives. What your mama didn't teach you is that this is true feminine power. Don't get me wrong, I'm not talking about the office! Please, be strong and focused at the office but then leave it there. I'm also not talking about being a pushover. Being empowered and mysterious comes from being more committed to yourself than anyone else. You want a man who cherishes, provides, and protects. If your date isn't interested in these things, he's a boy, not a man. Move on.

The Reluctant Princess

I was a tomboy. I never thought of myself as a princess. Princesses made me want to throw up. When I became engaged in 2006 and bought a wedding dress with a pink and ivory beaded halter, satin-ribbon-lined tulle bottom, and a pink bow in the back, let's just say I was shocked. Perhaps, subconsciously, I wanted to be a princess and to be saved. I didn't see it until that moment, staring at myself in a pool of pink and white. What I knew was my rebel. My rebel was very strong and would not give up her freedom for anything. These two worked against each other. Do you have a reluctant princess inside you, or an overzealous rebel?

Why Relationship?

I've been single for 48 years. I've garnered lots of dating experience and very few long-term relationships (and by long term, I mean, a year being the longest). I've always felt like a caged bird in relationship. I truly believed that a committed relationship would hold me back from living out my destiny, while simultaneously holding it up as the answer to all my problems. It reminds me of the aforementioned quote that my client sent to me; my grandiosity kept me single. No one was special enough, and I wasn't sure that I wanted anyone to see how not-special I actually felt in my day to day life.

So why a relationship? Why do you want a relationship, what is the purpose of relationship, and how do we set one up free of resentment? It's important to answer these questions because, even with the best intentions, your thought process can get muddled.

I recently thought I had fallen in love. This man showered me with love, affection, and gifts. He promised me everything a girl could ask for, and I believed it because I craved a change. I wanted to learn, grow, and expand. We moved quickly, moving in together and blending our families. However, he then revealed more of his essence, which was very different than mine. Our morals and values did not align, and we could not find a compromise, even with the help of a therapist. When this happens, there is only one thing to do: pull up your big girl pants, and make a decision that is best for you —move on.

Walls or Boundaries?

As children, we are often not taught how to set healthy boundaries. But healthy boundaries are key to any relationship being successful. If you are a strong and successful woman, you are most likely tough. Your toughness has gotten you this far and is awesome, but it can be a deterrent while dating. Ever wonder why the sweet, little girl type of women seem to always get the guy? We'll get to the bottom of the difference between walls and boundaries and how to let down the walls.

Owning the Wound

Rarely do I hear from my clients that their childhoods were filled with easy love. Everyone in the world is wounded. Learning to have compassion for our own wounding will free us up to have compassion for our date and partners. Later in this book, we will take a deeper look at the common wounding, how to own it, and how to use it as a source of empowerment.

Igniting the Magic

Vision boards and talismans have always left a bad taste in my mouth. I believe there is magic everywhere and anything can be turned into a mystical experience by setting clear intentions. With that being said, it was in 2017 that I decided for myself to find a relationship and infuse a few items with that intention to help me along. I'll share with you a few tricks that will keep your search for love fun and magical.

We are going to cover a lot of ground, creating a synergy for you to attract the right partner by going deep into the labyrinth of your soul, loving all those forgotten parts, bringing to light the best part of you, and reminding the hardened parts that *you* got this and you are co-creating a life that is extra, not one dictated by your subconscious.

We are all capable of creating expansive and amazing lives. We just have to get out of our own way.

Chapter 3: Open All the Doors and Windows, Sage the Place

We all just want to be loved. We want someone to hold our hand during each painful moment.

— Unknown

You'll find the 'one' when you aren't looking. We've all heard this one before. I distinctly remember saying to myself sometime in my late 20's, *I'm just going to focus on me and the rest will fall into place.* As you remember, by the time I was 30, I was freaking out. Nothing had fallen into place. All my friends were settling down and having kids and I was *single!* When something is meant to be, it's easy, but this doesn't mean you sit around reading self-help books, which don't really help anyone, and your guy is going to knock on your door. It also doesn't mean that if something comes into your life it's meant to be for forever. It's meant to be there until it's not anymore and if we trust our guts and live outside of fear, we'll be able to let go of what needs to be released.

I've ready many books on how to have a successful relationship, and they all loop back to you knowing yourself, speaking your truth, and having compassion for you and your partner. There is no avoiding the relationship you need to have with your *self.* It is the key to everything.

If you want a successful relationship, there is no better place to learn about yourself than through dating. If you 'take a break' to 'work on yourself' you are really just opting out, unless you are healing a broken heart.

If you are, then take the time. Broken hearts hurt, and you need to heal before stepping out again. I've heard it takes half the time you were together to heal, so if you've been single for years and the relationship only lasted a few months, its time start dating again.

You are perfect right now to find true love.

Dating

I wish I could wave my magic wand over you, dress you up, and hand you off to your prince, but that is just a fairy tale. And honestly? Maybe that prince sucked in bed or snored? Reality will come in at some point.

So let's find your real prince charming, the one who snores, farts, leaves his socks around, knocks his head on things, and might even have a traffic violation or two, but loves you like mad and believes his purpose on earth is to serve you. This might take a little longer, so it requires patience. If you want to settle, you can find a man in a month or two and start your family. It's easy, but this book is about finding your true love, without settling. This takes magic and patience.

Where to begin?

Online Dating Is For Everyone

Take a deep inhale, sigh it out and repeat after me, *online dating is fun*! This is your new mantra. Everything is what you make it. If you have a negative opinion of online dating, then you will have a negative experience of online dating.

You might be thinking, *I'm a very successful woman, I'm not going online*. I'd say this is just another way of you saying 'no' to the very thing you want. Everyone is online. I've worked with countless successful women and men who are all online. If dating online is really off-putting, then hire a service, but you need to be pro-active and ask them to set up dates often. I once spent thousands of dollars on a dating service, and they sent me out on three dates that were completely wrong for me.

How to make this whole thing fun?

There are so many apps out there, so find the one or two that work for you. Personally, I like Bumble because you can control who contacts you. However, you might like to be contacted first, so Tinder, Hinge, OKCupid or Plenty of Fish might work for you. I had been online dating for almost 20 years, so by the time Bumble came around and I no longer had to sift through a bunch of unwanted "hello's," it was a welcomed break.

A few tips on your profile:

- Include as many photos as you can, but try to limit the overtly sexy ones (you'll attract the wrong kind of man)
- Include at least one, if not more, full body shots (men are visual creatures).
- No pics of friends, limit the pets, no babies

- Write a blurb in your voice with your sense of humor and specifics about you. Everyone likes to laugh, travel, dinners out, and is looking for a 'partner in crime.'

What makes a profile stand out is the specific information that makes you, you. What makes you laugh? Where's your favorite place to eat? What kind of food? Don't be afraid to put that you are looking for a committed relationship.

Once you've got your profile up, you are ready to begin swiping. Stay open and excited. I suggest to all my clients that they not read profiles first. For the first round, just swipe left or right based on your gut and level of attraction. Keep it easy. Learn to trust yourself. I remember one time, just for fun, I swiped right on every guy. I was amazed by who had swiped right on me too. But let's just say, I didn't reach out to many of them.

Once you're mutually matched, read the guy's profile and take another look at his pictures. If you are on Bumble and like what he says or feel there's something interesting about him, reach out. If you decide to reach out, find something in their profile that you can ask them about. If they have nothing on their profile, say something smart and funny about it. Keep it light. Be the person you'd want to date.

If you are on an app where the guys can reach out to you, wait. Do not reach out. Wait for him to reach out. I don't care how hot he is, or if you feel he's *the one*. Sit on your hands and wait. If a man doesn't reach out or respond back to you, move on emotionally and intellectually. You don't have to 'un-match' the match, that's too dramatic. Just let it hang out there and you move on with men and dates who are actually showing up.

Decide for yourself how long you are willing to be pen pals, but do not ask a guy out or hint towards getting a coffee, always leave it to them unless you want to be the man in the relationship, always making plans, etc. Your man will be asking for your phone number and asking you without you giving it a second thought. That's how men work. Online dating is leaving a door open. It doesn't mean it's the only way to find a man, continue to go out, etc, but why not get a lot of practice in? You will learn so much about yourself.

In-Person Dating

Once upon a time, people met in bars, through friends, at coffee shops, and men were bold enough to ask you out if you held eye contact with them. This can and does still happen but it happens less often. In fact, the last time I heard of two people meeting in person was after they had seen each other on the dating apps and the guy knew my client was single. Ha!

Continue to go out, tell your friends you're dating, etc., but also keep online dating.

All dating is good for you. It's just 'duty dating' as coined by Dr. Pat Allen, which means you are dating men that you might not have a huge spark with to learn about what exactly you want in a man.

Quick Tips to Avoid Dating Pitfalls

If you are pursuing the man, stop! I know that this is easy to say but harder to put into practice. But I promise that you will enjoy how good it feels to be pursued once you start practicing this step. It will also bolster your self-worth. Unless you are looking to be the masculine energy in your relationship and you prefer a feminine energy guy, in which case you should feel free to pursue. How you set up the relationship in the beginning is the foundation of the relationship. It's very hard to shift this once you are in it. The only hard and fast rule about all of this is not to settle.

How to know if you are settling

This comes up all the time with my clients. Sometimes a few warning signs can be confused with you settling, but the energy of the two is very different. One has no spark, no excitement. It lacks passion. Throughout my dating history I have dated guys that lacked a spark, but I dated them anyway to see if it would come (it never did). You want to be excited, turned on, scared, and curious when you meet a man.

Falling in love with a phantom.

You are a busy woman with a full life. Unless the guy is showing up (and by that I mean he's inviting you out, calling, texting, bringing you flowers and gifts), don't think about him. It's an energy suck and will leave you exhausted. Go on with your bad self — your *man* will not leave you wondering. He'll be on you, not able to get enough of you. Obsessing means you are in fantasy and trying to convince the universe that this your man. It never works. He's a phantom. Move on.

I once had a client that spoke about this 'boyfriend' of hers, but they never went out. He was very busy getting his PhD and was mostly unavailable. She hung on to the thought of him because having a guy that could get together every once in a while was still better than nothing in her mind.

After working with me about a month, she broke up with him and started dating, longing for something real.

Respond in Kind

When you are not sure of what to say, respond in kind. Meaning you match your energy to the energy the guy is putting out. If you can't get a read of how much the he likes you, or if you aren't sure how you are feeling, respond in kind to keep the communication going until you are more certain. Then wait for him to ask you out or hint that you'd like to be asked out by saying something like, what really turns me on is when a man takes charge. If he takes charge, he might be good candidate, but if he doesn't respond or comes back with a weak response, he's probably not your man.

Loving Bad Boys, aka Narcissists

I could write a whole book on just this topic alone. I used to joke that if 10 guys walked into the room, I'd pick the one unavailable bad boy. I never quite shook this tendency.

In my coaching groups, we often say that we are "rewiring" the vagina to be attracted to good guys. Duty dating is your best friend if this your issue. You will need to rewire what you are attracted to.

Remember Ken and the grapefruit? I showed up like a child and he was my mean father. Why? Because whatever your childhood, unless you've done some deep unpacking, you will equate the feeling most associated with love to how you were loved by your parents. Without knowing, it you will seek this feeling out in partnership, hoping to heal the wound of not being good enough, worthy enough, needing someone to stay not to feel abandoned.

It's a crazy cycle and almost impossible to shift completely. Its deep soul work, shifting karma, and having enough challenging experiences that hopefully you begin to be attracted to different type of man. You can too. We all are worthy of love, right now. Just be ready because when you meet a man who loves you for you, it's going to feel very uncomfortable.

Know What You Want

If you are reading this book, it's clear that you want relationship and you don't want to settle. But you need to know that, by dating, you will meet many men, and sometimes you will want different things from different men.

At one point, I had what I called a trifecta boyfriend: one man who played the role of the lover, the next guy was the unavailable man that I was trying not to fall in love with, and the third guy was an old friend that I hoped I might end up with. It worked for a while, but in the end it was unfulfilling. I wanted to be all in and in love with someone who felt the same way.

I recently had a client tell me after a first date that she felt an energetic sludge like residue after meeting her date. It felt a little suspect to me because by the way she described him, he sounded like a good guy for her for the moment, but her perception of him was clouded. A week later, she texted to say that she had slept with him, and the sex was liberating. She saw him differently than their first meeting.

The first thing I suggested was that she define this relationship for herself. I asked her what she wanted from this guy. She was stumped. She went on with a few excuses about why she couldn't really think of him as relationship material.

Interestingly, she said, "I know sleeping with him felt right, whereas in the past, I often did it out of obligation. I like him, he's super funny, I feel totally myself around him, we have chemistry, and I could see us dating."

Are you curious to know what her excuses were? Well, he was going through a divorce and is re-building his career. When seeking relationship, those two things are easily fixed. The way your soul feels with a man is the mana of relationship. Find this first, see if the man continues to show up, and the rest will slowly fall into place with patience. If not being fully divorced is a deal breaker for you, no problem, just trust your intuition.

He Knows What He Wants

A man knows what he wants. If he's treating you like a one-night-stand, that's the place you hold in his life. If you want to avoid this trap, hold yourself to a higher esteem and don't sleep with him until you know him or you trust that he has deeper feelings for you. I once dated a man who had swiped past my profile for a year before swiping right on me. He wasn't ready for something real and he sensed I'd be something real. He continued to date, acquiring quite a harem. When I met him, he had three women hanging around, hoping it would soon be their time to be his girlfriend, but their time was never going to come. Their role in his life had been established. It wasn't going to change. He committed to me immediately, and I was his treasure.

An Available Man Doesn't Stay Available for Long

Even if you are having a bad week or you don't hear from someone, you should be super excited to keep going. The good guys, the available guys, don't stay on dating apps for long. They are seeking partnership, are available, and they are not afraid. They get snatched up quickly. Like I said, I'd been on-line dating for around 15 years, and I've seen the same guys on the dating apps for 15 years.

About two years ago, I had a man reach out to me, very excited to get to know me better. He was freshly separated, not quite divorced, a family man. And guess what I told him? I told him to reach out once he was divorced. I laugh now at my arrogance and grandiosity. For whatever reason he friended me on Facebook and soon after I saw he had started dating a beautiful woman. And just last week, I saw pictures of their wedding on social media.

I was happy for him, and it taught me a lot about pushing people away too quickly. My fear was about me, not him. I wasn't ready. Please learn from this, available men do not stay available for long.

Stay Curious!

'Stay curious' could be another mantra. You're not going to have chemistry with every guy you meet. But thinking that you need to have chemistry on every date is too much pressure to put on yourself anyway. However, I believe every person on earth has enough of an interesting story to sit and have a cup of coffee with. If you are on a date and you think it's boring, my bet is your own attitude made it so. Instead, draw the story out of the guy. You bring life to life. Once I went out with a guy who I was pretty sure was either homeless or down on his luck, but there was something about him that peaked my curiosity. I wasn't wrong. He arrived in dirty board shorts, and even though it was quite clear that he had less money than me, he insisted on paying for my tea.

His story was fascinating. He worked at the front desk of a yoga studio and had traveled through India several times on spiritual quests. Before he gave up everything to seek enlightenment, he worked in the tech world. He gave it all up to find God but was still lost and was now bitter because the god he was looking for did not show up. He thought he was going to have that spiritual seeker's happy ending, but instead he ended up broke and homeless. While it didn't work out with this man, we kept in touch for a few months and I still think about his story today.

The lesson here is that, when looking for true love, keep all doors and windows open and a little sage never hurt anyone. You are looking for one man. It doesn't matter how many men it takes to get you there.

Chapter 4: Addicted to Fantasy

Your fantasies have to die in order for your dreams to come true.

— *Breck Costin*

One doesn't often think of fantasy as a problem, but it actually can stop you from achieving your dreams and finding love. How?

Fantasy is living in your head. It is, "a state where you are addicted to the outcome as an answer to a self-worth issue," according to Breck Costin, my life coach for several years. How does this show up?

I once coached a woman, a fellow coach, who wanted to be the next Oprah. It's easy to see how that would solve a self-worth issue. Her passion wasn't about actually helping people, it was to be discovered by Oprah and then to become the next Oprah. I didn't coach her very long because she couldn't see the truth of her self. She defended her point of view, which was based in fantasy and ego.

Back in 2009, I wrote the following in my journal. It was probably a *Law of Attraction* exercise, as that was *everything* back then. I've included it here:

March 11, 2009

I am living a life of true liberation, and I am blessed. I am a healer and have a small haven,   an oasis where people gather to experience peace.

I have an amazing husband, who also lives from a place of freedom. We are blessed with   our children, love, emotional bliss, joy, travel, freedom, gratefulness, and the sun.

My day unfolds naturally, with loving guidance from spirit and all. I have all the money I   need and want.

My husband is of substance. He is handsome, and we have fantastic chemistry, a slight   touch from him and I'm fully awake — this   connection   comes   from   a   wonderful   and   healthy   emotional bond where our first concern is the happiness of each other. We don't drink   except wine on occasion, no smoking or drugs. We are grateful for what we have found   and   treasure   it. I know exactly what to say when he is down —with a touch, a smile, he   knows he is loved and feels like the luckiest man in the world to have me (and he is) and I   am   the   luckiest   woman   alive   to   have him.

With this beautiful life and relationship I also know that I know nothing and will listen to   the guidance of Spirit in every moment of my day.

I   have   given   up   the   right   to   ever   have   a   successful relationship and there is where freedom   presides.

Dream or fantasy? It's a little tricky, right? A lot of this has come to fruition, so one would guess dream, but on closer inspection it was pure fantasy. It was all in my head.

Another favorite quote of mine from Breck is, *dreams are taking action from the purest part of yourself.* I had created this particular fantasy (there's been many) because it made me believe I'd feel loved, validated, smart, and finally good enough. Yes, it's a beautiful vision for a life, but at the time the only action I was taking to make it happen was working on my *self.* That work was even steeped in a false sense of self, meaning that I thought I was *special* and that I could have my dreams come true without getting uncomfortable or working. I had yet to learn how to incorporate my wounding.

I was afraid of making real change and the fantasy kept me safe and in *hope.* It became a habit, an escape, an addiction. The idea of *someday* or *when/then* was how I kept myself thinking I was doing *something,* and reading self-help books supported the fantasy.

Here are some other examples of fantasy:

- When I have $10,000 in the bank, then I'll be happy.
- When I lose weight, then I'll do yoga.
- When I have time, then I'll write.
- When I've created the perfect little alter, then I'll meditate.
- When I sell my memoir, then I'll meet a man and be happy.

- When he/she sees how amazing I am, then they will fall in love with me.
- When he/she gets divorced, then we'll be together.
- Someday (when everything aligns), I'll quit my job and follow my heart.
- Someday the perfect idea for a script will come in, and then I'll write.
- Someday I'll be Oprah, and then I'll feel worthy.
- Someday I'll wake up and feel differently about my husband/wife, and then I'll be happy.

In fantasy, you don't have to go through the fear, loneliness, second guessing, and hardship that creating a dream takes. That's why there are so few people living their actual dreams.

In that excerpt from my journal there is so much focus on the man because I believed this man would find me and I'd have this ideal life because of him, like a miracle. I never saw myself doing it on my own.

I remember the moment it became crystal clear that I was addicted to fantasy. It was about 6 months after I wrote that entry in my journal, a casual Saturday morning. I was doing laundry, pulling clothes from the washer and putting them in the dryer, and had the thought, *someday when Ken walks through that door, he's going to tell me he loves me and then everything will feel better, I just know it.*

I froze when I heard the thought. This line of thinking was keeping me stuck. I wasn't dating. I was miserable and in denial of the truth that Ken really didn't give a shit about me and on top of that, I was in fantasy that he was going to show up and love me like in some romantic comedy. Obviously, myself worth issue of not being good enough was going to be resolved with his declaration of love and fairy tale ending.

Ken's death was a wakeup call. Because I didn't know of his death for several months after he had died, I had been living in fantasy, thinking he'd come back. When I discovered his death, I had to mourn him on multiple levels, the reality of him and the fantasy of him that I had been carrying all that time. I realized that, even though my relationship with Ken was over, I had held on to the fantasy that one day we would show up. He'd call or knock on my door, chase me down the aisle on my wedding day to another man, and profess his love to me. I had been … delusional.

But I wasn't alone. I was not the only *victim* of Ken. There were other fair maidens out there touched by Ken's magic, like maidens drawn to Orpheus's music. They, too, believed that one day Orpheus would enter Hades to retrieve them, fooled by the sorcery of his music. But there can only be one Eurydice. Back when I discovered his death, I found myself staring at a painting of Orpheus leading Eurydice through the woods. The fair maidens watched from across the water in mourning, saddened that they had not been chosen. What they did not know was Eurydice was being led unknowingly to her death; lost in him, in a trance. In all the paintings of Eurydice there is no joy — only pain, suffering and longing. Rejection is oftentimes a blessing.

I would come to find out that Ken was a bit of scoundrel and was dating multiple people, unable and unwilling to commit, living a web of secrets and lies that I ignored because the fantasy felt better to me. What I really needed to do was break up with him and feel the sadness, fear, and pain of it all.

Now, after years of real work on myself and taking incredible risks, I'd say what I wrote in my journal is a dream. I can see myself creating an oasis for people to find peace and healing, or doing humanitarian work on a larger scale. It has taken almost 10 years to create this vision with lots of tears, failures, and a few private tantrums.

The vision I created did not take into account that my wounding would challenge my any relationship I entered into, which is what kept me out of relationship, because I was not willing to get uncomfortable and be vulnerable.

The year before I met my current boyfriend, I had done so much internal heavy lifting that I was dating from a place of an emotionally mature woman, not from my not good enough little girl, where fantasy fed the fairy tale. Fantasy was gone. I knew the work that a solid relationship would take.

The week I found out Ken passed away, I wrote the following.

St. Joan of Arc

I hear the voice of God
And I want to save people

And in it I sacrifice myself.

Ken, I feel the abuse you had as a child, I felt my mother's abuse.

I just want to save them and I hear the voice of God.

All is forgiven, forgive your selves.
I will not be rescued
My prince is not coming
There is no fantasy to sustain me.
I am what I have, that and God.

I can do this.
I can do this.

I can esteem myself.
I can have healthy boundaries.
I can have self worth if I have nothing.

Perhaps you have a few fantasies kicking around that are keeping you from stepping into the reality of relationship. I have found that clients are often looking for something that doesn't exist. Yes, the spark has to be there, but the man will not be perfect. Perfection is a fantasy and will keep you alone.

Pull up your sleeves and enjoy the trenches of imperfection. Find out where you are still stuck in fantasy.

Chapter 5: What Your Mama Didn't Teach You

Within every woman there is a wild and natural creature, a powerful force, filled with good instincts, passionate creativity, and ageless knowing.

— *Clarissa Pinkola Estés*

I sat on the bus, watching my sister make out with the boy that I had been romantically involved with just weeks ago; tongues lashing about, hands groping, no attempt to be discreet, or careful that maybe I'd be watching. I was a freshman in high school. She was a senior. He was a junior. It was a confusing and vulnerable time and watching them, right there in front of me, and it broke my heart. Daav was the first boy in high school that I had become smitten with, and who had shown a mutual interest. We 'dated' (as much as it could be called dating) for a few weeks. We didn't have an official break up, and I don't even think we kissed. His attention made me nervous, so I found myself tongue-tied when he called and avoiding eye contact when he passed by at school. I was a mess. My sister swooped in and took him with her confidence and predatory focus.

This painful experience, along with other experiences of women treating me badly, took me right out of the sisterhood. I didn't trust women after that. I did everything to avoid groups of women. In my 20's I was wild — if there was a committed man I was attracted to, I'd still go for it. Usually, I'd get him through sex and, being the 'party girl,' I would offer up what I thought he wanted —freedom and fun. I figured he wouldn't be looking around if he was happy with his girlfriend. I thought of myself as a courtesan or a mistress and I loved the role. It was powerful, and I felt special.

Looking back, I was not special. I was sad. I was being used. I had created a reality that was the farthest thing from the truth of feminine power. I was a wounded little girl, and I saw the domesticated woman as weak and tame. I wanted nothing to do with her, and yet I yearned deeply to be loved and to be special to someone. I resented this type of domesticated woman.

Being in the sisterhood is a huge part of finding love. Through the years, it became apparent that men will accept sex if it's offered. It does not make you special and has nothing to do with love. Pursuing another woman's man screams *I am hurting*. I truly believe there is not a more difficult role on earth than wife and mother, especially for us wild ones. It is to be honored and respected.

My mother never taught me about sisterhood or about how to have a successful relationship. I had to learn what it meant to be a part of the sisterhood, to be a woman who wasn't desperately trying to prove herself for a man's love. So, learn what your mama never taught ya. Make mistakes, speak your truth, and strive to be honored and respected.

Sit On The Lotus Flower

I once dated a guy who had a harem of women. I am not joking. At any given time he could call up three or four women and they would party with him and have sex with him. It was illuminating to see myself from the other side and how pathetic it actually looked. This man was to these women, what Ken had been to me, they hung on every word, picked up his children from school, dog sat, and babysat, desperately hoping he'd finally see them as good enough be his girlfriend.

So why did this handsome *player* pic me? Because I sat fully in my power and did not budge. My relationship with my *self* was the most important thing, and I would not sacrifice it for anything. If I lose my self than I can't work. My intuition comes from my connection to my higher self. If I have noise in my head or feel disconnected, I cannot hear the intuitive information the Universe wants to share with me to give to my clients.

I remember one of the first times I spent the night with this handsome player, he asked me to make his children breakfast in the morning. What? I was blown away. I thought, *this dude must be used to having some weak ass women around if he thinks I'm going to get up and make his kids breakfast the second night we spend together while he lounges in bed.* My answer was no.

He had me confused for a desperate woman that would do anything for love. If my saying no was a deal breaker for him, best to get that out of the way now so we could both move on. *Sitting on the lotus flower* means speaking your truth and knowing by speaking your truth you will find a man that will love you for YOU. If you are a people pleaser a man will never get the opportunity to love you, he will just date your people pleasing qualities until he gets bored of you or tired of your built up resentments.

I often tell clients that a relationship doesn't really begin until you ask for something. Only then will you see how the person is going to show up for you. This man got that lesson when he asked me to make his kids breakfast. I said no, which was my truth. I was a single mom, and I was looking for true partnership, not to be of service to a man and his children. Such a request on our first or second sleepover was definitely a red flag, and if I had said yes *to win his love*, I would have set up the relationship as me servicing him. And that was not what I was looking for.

You can see how far I'd come from the days of eating grapefruit to win Ken's love. I was in reality, no longer in fantasy. I did paint that red flag white, but sometimes you need to step into a relationship to see the truth of yourself.

I recently had a client reach out to me, worried that if she stated her needs of wanting more communication with her boyfriend she would appear needy. I told her, "He doesn't know how you're feeling. You need to tell him and see how he shows up."

It was clear she had over compromised herself and was disappearing in the relationship to 'not make waves.' "I'll have to get off my lotus flower," she responded.

She thought that, by sharing her feelings, she was being weak and off her lotus flower, but it's the exact opposite. You share your feelings and if the man wishes to cherish you, he'll hear you and show up to please.

My response to her was, "No, you are still on your lotus flower, you aren't chasing him, you are just making requests from a place of power."

That's what being a majestic fully empowered woman looks like. It's not withholding, martyrdom, or saying yes, when you mean no.

F*** The Rules

When you are dating from a queenlike feminine power, there are no rules because you are making conscious choices and are the victim of nothing.

Have you been tying yourself up in a knot, trying to follow the various rules that dating books suggest? I remember thinking that if I followed all the rules, I would magically find love. It didn't work. All the knowledge I gained from all the books on relationship and dating helped for sure, but there was no quick and/or easy fix. I had to dig deep and break up subconscious patterns.

Remember my trifecta boyfriend? My three men that fulfilled different roles to create the sum of the perfect boyfriend?

The first man was a longtime friend. I had known him since I was 18. I met him in college and was smitten with him from the first time I laid eyes on him. When I'd bump into him at coffee shops, I couldn't speak to him much like how I showed up with Daav, the guy my sister swooped up after me. Eventually, after working on several plays together (we were both theater majors) we became very good friends. We have traveled back and forth from LA to Seattle more times than I can remember. Throughout the 30 years of friendship, he's played an important part in many of my more pivotal memories. We've only kissed once, but our relationship always felt like it teetered on the edge of being something more. We had grown accustom to talking on the phone at least once a week for 2 hours or more. He's always felt like a husband from a different lifetime. In the trifecta, he played the role of the long term partner by giving me unconditional love, intellectual stimulation, emotional support, and a deep knowing of my soul.

The second man in the triad was a cowboy. We did similar work by facilitating equine assisted learning. I sent him a friend request on Facebook, and he called me soon after and asked if I wanted to go for a ride with him (yes, I did). He was handsome and sexy. I soon realized after he asked me out that I had seen him at a Buck Brannaman clinic and was totally attracted to him because of his horsemanship skills and leading-man good looks. I even attempted to meet him after the clinic but to no avail.

On that first ride, each time our knees touched, electric currents sparked my entire body. I was out of my mind for this guy. One week later, we hooked up, and it was hot and steamy. I hadn't felt this way for a long time, too long. Something had awakened in me and I wanted more, but I wouldn't get it. I would soon discover that he was unavailable.

Wanting him and not getting him was torturous for me, but also completely illuminating. For a whole year I worked next to him, facilitating groups in recovery, which completely turned me on sexually although I was not able to do anything about it. I never felt good enough, and I was always trying to prove myself worthy of his love, often tongue tied. It was the perfect set up for me to heal, and I did.

I broke the *monkey dance* routine I had learned so well as a child when trying to get my father's love. This was what was keeping me from finding true love in my life.

The final man was my lover. Since I could not have sex with the man I was passionately 'falling in love with,' I needed to find release somewhere. I met my lover online, and we both agreed that we only wanted to be lovers. I'm not sure why or how this happened, but it was organic and easy. It started with coffee in a public place, and we chatted for over an hour before we went back to my place. It was fun and surprising. He was kind, smart, funny and helped me open up to having a man in my life. I remember the first time he was naked in my kitchen, I thought to myself, *there's a naked man in my kitchen, and it feels all right.*

I didn't need to do the *monkey dance* with him. He'd show up, we'd make love in the middle of the day, and he'd leave. We never went out, and we only had one sleep over, which was wonderful. Unfortunately, it also happened to be the last time I saw him. Maybe it was just too much intimacy for two people not wanting to commit to one another? I don't know. Sometimes we'd do yoga together in my bungalow or have lunch. It was romantic and gentle and probably not what one thinks of when they think about a *lover*.

Finding love is a deeply personal and romantic experience with one's self. The more you are able to sit in your power, the more you are able to make choices that best serve you and the healing you so need.

Let A Man be a Man

For strong, successful women, the difference between being feminine versus being mothering can be confusing. Not just that, but when you are a strong, masculine woman who kicks ass in the office, you need to figure out how to bring the 'her' on dates. A man doesn't want to date a man, he wants a woman; a mysterious and powerful woman who he's not sure what to do with or what she's thinking or feeling. This is the secret to being unforgettable and wanted.

I recently had a client reach out via text about a guy she'd been dating and really liked. They had tentative plans to get together that night. He'd been fairly busy (she was preparing to leave town for two weeks the next day) and had had to cancel a couple other tentative dates. So, she was wondering if she should text him and let him know that she'd like an answer about hanging out by 7pm? Her energy was needy and willing to be a doormat for this guy. I told her that he needs 'a hand slap,' and to let him know that 8pm was getting too late because she was leaving the next day, but that she was bummed because she really wanted to see him.

This is a simple statement of her needs and feelings.

She didn't like what I had asked her to write, it felt uncomfortable. The number one truth of change is that it's uncomfortable. She came back to me and stated that she instead wanted 'closure' or 'clarity' from him, so she'd know whether to keep in touch or close the door while she was on her trip. She had completely lost touch with her feminine, empowered woman and was fully in her masculine energy, trying to control and know the outcome. She had forgotten herself.

My response via text was:

Nope! That's masculine. Be a woman. He's not a business deal. Its romance. If you are leaving town for two weeks, then closure is not in the picture. Unless you want to hear its over because he's going to keep dating and making out with other women, and I don't think you want to hear that. Keep it loose, be feminine, keep going with your life, see if he shows up, if he doesn't, keep moving on...you are awesome and if he's not ready for your awesomeness move on...

She eventually sent the text to saying exactly what I had instructed her to write. He said he felt bummed as well. It was her first step to knowing her worth and speaking from a place of being an empowered woman. A man will string you along if you let him. Don't let him. Know your value and don't try to control him or the situation to feel safe.

Romance isn't *safe,* it's vulnerable. A man who really wants you, will show up and this is key for a man you want to start a family with. There is nothing worse than having a children with a partner who is absent and unkind.

My client and the guy texted a couple times while she was away. She wanted to reach out when she got back, and I told her not to. Shortly after, he texted her. She texted me, thanking me because she got to feel wanted, and if he had only been responding to her text, she would have felt small and needy.

By sharing your emotional needs and desires, by not being a yes-woman, or trying to control the outcome, you create a mystery around yourself and men love a mystery. It creates torque in the relationship, and there is nothing better for a relationship than torque. Torque creates a bonding tension and tension creates passion.

This is what you will want because once you and your man are committed and then married, the passion will be what keeps you together through raising children when things can get a little tricky.

Chapter 6: Reluctant Princess

Some people get lost for so long they forget what it was like to be themselves.

— Anonymous

I wonder how often we force our feet into glass slippers that don't fit, just to make our fairy tales come true? Especially if our fairytale includes children and our clock is ticking. If you wish to settle with a man to have children, no problem — but you must make this decision consciously. It is unfair to punish the man you choose to do this with down the road. Dig deep.

Sometimes we get so far away from ourselves that we forget who we are, and this becomes a self-worth issue. Everything becomes more fun when we become the heroine of our own story and are able to see life as a grand adventure, in which there is no settling.

We are only victims if we choose to be. We can make our lives what we want. But I also understand that this is so much easier said than done because, unfortunately, we all have deep wounds within that are covered in tough scar tissue. This creates subconscious patterns that then run our lives. The image or personality we display to the outer world protects our wounds and keeps us from our true selves and deprives us of our self-worth because we are always trying to please or prove.

The No-Current

As you have gathered, I have desperately wanted a relationship with a loving partner without settling. I spent my life trying to find this illusive person. It was my deepest desire, but no matter how hard I tried, it didn't happen.

I'd done enough work on myself to know that there were many factors as to why I was so challenged and couldn't seem to find a relationship. Some of these being: caged bird syndrome, parents got divorced, never had a healthy relationship mirrored to me, love avoidant, love addict, co-dependent, fear of fulfillment, not deserving of happiness, etc. No matter how much I read and intellectually understood, it never changed. I was still single.

At the time, I could easily imagine this relationship in a faraway fantasy, and if felt good, easy, and fulfilling. However, while living in the fantasy, I did not take into consideration the human imperfections of all concerned. I did not bring into account the necessary change, adjustment, and relinquishing required of a real relationship.

When I finally sat down and thought about a relationship coming into my life with all the reality I could muster, I felt sick. I imagined this 'dream man' with my son, asking for my time, wanting to do things with me, spending the night with me every week, and I felt like throwing up. It was too much.

A huge knot gripped my belly. I teetered on having a panic attack. Even though this was something I'd wanted with all my heart, I had a big *no-current* running through me when I actually thought about getting it in reality.

Discovering this feeling completely changed my life. It woke me up to a new reality. For the first time, I *got it* on a soul level that I was blocking my own way. This discoveries led me away from thinking I was being punished or rewarded by a higher power and the equally false idea that there was no order, or no superior intelligence in the universe.

When I first discovered that I was saying *no*, I was beyond disappointed, but then a sense of empowerment came in. I no longer felt unlucky or inferior. I was able to take full responsibility for my no-current, and it changed everything.

Once I learned to recognize and feel the subtle and once remote no, everything began to shift. I had always felt that my attitude towards wanting a relationship was positive but looking back there was always an urgent, frantic, hopeless *yes* clamoring, crying, and trembling beneath the surface. Why? Because the undetected no-current was defeating all my efforts. I actually had a fear that I would never meet the guy, even though my *yes* seemed to be all *yes*.

This is the *no-current* doing its dirty work. Once my yes-current was able to observe my no-current without judgment, what was once vague and confused became concise. The no-current had blurred my memory of past victories, leaving me feeling powerless. It kept me from figuring out my own confusions, unanswered questions, and vague uneasy feelings in a concise way.

I wasn't able to tackle these blocks as they barricaded the way, or ask for help, or cultivate my inner will to see the truth behind what was stopping me and be willing to change. But this all stopped with the awareness and observation of the no-current.

I began to register my inner *no's* with the intent to see and understand the truth throughout my day. I'd find them in the haze of half-conscious thoughts, the vague and diffuse attitudes and expressions that are almost second nature and so easily overlooked. These half-conscious thoughts created very subtle reactions, which were key to who I really was. This is where I needed to pay attention, it was where the gold presided.

Opening myself up to the truth of my no-current was a decisive step toward bringing myself, my personality, into the yes-current. By doing this, I began to see how I pushed away, or withdrew from the very thing I desired. The no-current will weaken just by you observing it.

Not too long ago, I had a client come to me determined to be in relationship within 6 months. I liked her determination but was also aware that if this was something she really wanted, she'd have it, so there had to be no-current in there. After working with me for a bit, she discovered she had a hatred for men.

As you may imagine, it's hard to attract your true love when you carry the secret that you hate men. Her new-found awareness of hating men opened up an opportunity to shift perspectives. What was once in the dark and in the labyrinth of her subconscious was now brought to the light of her consciousness. After this discovery, the way my client dated became very different. She was open to the complexity of men and stopped projecting and transferring her subconscious attitudes on the to the guys, giving her the opportunity to see the reality of them.

When this kind of shift happens, your no-current cannot stay the same, it must change. Everything you need to know about yourself can be discovered in the layer between conscious thought and unconscious thought. The half-conscious material also comprises your fantasy life. Take a moment to notice your emotional reaction to both, and you will see the discrepancies, contradictions, and (more importantly) your immature expectations.

Inner Child

You might be thinking, *oh no not inner child crap,* but bear with me. The inner child is a goldmine of information. Maybe your inner child is wild and you have tried to bury her, being a good girl? Or perhaps she's a nerdy little thing that didn't have friends, and now you are trying to be cool so no one sees you're just a frightened little girl?

Remember the cowboy I was dating that was part of my boyfriend triad? Every time I was around him, I was so nervous, trying to prove I was worthy of love, it actually drove my conscious self nuts. I had no idea what was going on. I turned into a little girl around this man — doing things wrong, fumbling around, until I realized it was my inner child needing approval.

I had become so tough, needing to do everything right, handling everything, having control, that I was angry at this wounded little girl inside me for not being good enough. Subconsciously, I blamed her neediness, sadness, and insecurity for me not finding partnership.

Once I came to understand this, not just understand it but *feel* it in a flood of tears, I was able to heal. Remember, once something is brought to light, it must change.

I was able to sit with my inner child, love her, hold her, accept her wounding, and have complete compassion for her. After I did this, everything shifted. I was able to be around the cowboy and no longer needed his approval. I stood for myself and my own little girl and finally showed up like a woman. It was quite magical.

What does your little girl need? What are you able to give her so she can integrate and become one with you? Close your eyes, take a few deep breaths, and see where she appears.

Rebel

When I was 19, I traveled to Amsterdam by myself. It was my first time flying alone without my family. Before then, I might have been on a plane twice. My family often drove on our vacations. You'd think that traveling by myself for the first time might insight some fear, but when I looked it up in my journal, this is instead what I found.

August 15, 1989

I got into Amsterdam around 10pm and sweated around the airport. I had not a fucking   idea where I was going or what I was

*doing. Finally, I realized how to exit. I found my   way to the train
to discover I need guilders. I get guilders. Go to get my ticket and
find out   I can't leave for Paris until 7am the next morning. I
meet this 50 something year old guy,.   Helmut Schulze, a gem
dealer who ends up taking care of me. We walk around Amsterdam
        all night.*

This always makes me laugh. First, I don't even mention
fear. I never say, *I'm afraid!* Of course I wouldn't, because that
would be admitting to being weak. It would be allowing my inner
little girl to have a voice, which was too frightening. I was tough. I
didn't want anyone to see that inside I was a frightened young
woman that had no idea what she was doing.

I couldn't even admit fear to myself in the most sacred space
of my journal. Why? Because I had no idea it was an issue. This was
just how I was in the world, this is how I survived. Wasn't everyone
tough? Wasn't everyone doing things that scared the shit out of
them? Wasn't this 'normal?'

The thing is, what I remembered most about this story was
that I was such a non-conformist that when I exited the plane and
saw everyone going in one direction, I thought, *I'm going in the
opposite direction.* How dumb is that?

But this is the very trait that kept me out of a relationship.

My greatest fear was ending up in the suburbs with a
husband, and kids. It felt like a coffin. Once I was able to see that my
fear was keeping me from opening up to the possibility of meeting

someone available and loving, I made the conscious decision to step slowly into emotional space, cradling my fear and having compassion for myself.

Slowly, my rebel has calmed down, not so angry, able to love openly without walls, but it was not pretty at first. I describe it as bird caught in a house, flying into the windows.

Coming to terms with all these different aspects will free you up to find love. Your inner child and your rebel will occur differently than mine, but discovering them and getting real with them will help you to realize what is holding you back from living a fulfilled life.

This is not a process you do once and then you're done. As you grow and evolve, these inner archetypes need hand holding. At times when you feel not yourself or you are not sure why you are having the reaction that you are, check in. I can't imagine a better way to show love for yourself. It is also one of the greatest gifts you can give your children.

Until you integrate these different aspects of yourself it will be challenging to be the most beautiful woman in the world, which is what you will be to your true love. So best you see yourself as this first with all your emotional scars. It will make falling in love so much easier. Don't settle for a man who is not able to hold your inner child and handle your rebel. Maybe at the moment you are not seeing yourself as a queen, but I promise that you are one. And if you accept a man out of desperation and hope to change him, your glass slippers will cut your feet.

The prince charming fairy tale has created a world of hobbling women. Please do not become one of them.

Chapter 7: Relationship Is A Privilege

Truth is everybody is going to hurt you; you just gotta find the ones worth suffering for.

— Bob Marley

I love this quote by Bob Marley because it hits the truth of relationships on the head and doesn't play into a fairy tale idea of romance that we too often buy into as young girls. Really, what is suffering? Suffering is the gap between how we want things to be and how they are, which is part of falling in love. Both people are only seeing the best part of the other, the fantasy, and if we are willing to 'suffer' through this gap with another person, then perhaps we will end up in the same place. (Luckily, our brain chemistry helps, too, with hits of dopamine, serotonin, oxytocin, and endorphins, allowing us to feel good).

The caveat here is that one partner cannot be suffering alone for it to be considered true, reciprocal love. When you suffer alone, nothing real is happening in a relationship — you are just spinning your wheels of denial and fantasy. You could spend weeks caught in a state of fantasy before realizing that your partner either isn't that invested in the fantasy, or they are just unable to see it themselves. As they say, it it takes two to tango, and if your partner isn't even on the dance floor, then its time to move on. Nothing is happening,.

It is said that the key to a successful relationship is communication, but if we are lying to ourselves about ourselves then how can communication in our relationship be anything but a lie? This is the very reason why knowing yourself, truly knowing yourself with all the good, all the bad, the dark and twisty, and being willing to share it with someone else is the first commitment in a relationship.

Your inner purpose is to be kind to yourself, to adore yourself, and to sanctify yourself. Resolve yourself to this and you will dissolve yourself, which is the deepest love you will ever know. The next commitment in relationship is for you to be kind to your partner, adore your partner, and sanctify your partner and the partnership.

Why Relationship?

When we are single, all we 'want' is a relationship, but now we've learned that if we were really an all-in (a *hell yeah* kind of all-in) we'd have a relationship. So something is stopping us from fully embracing our desire for partnership. Maybe re-defining relationship is all we need to flip it on its head.

What is the purpose of relationship?

To heal. Partnership is to heal. My world opened up after the idea fully sank in, and I let go of the fantasy that the relationship was going to be easy enough to glide into and live happily after. By choosing to heal, I had to let go of the fantasy of being saved.

If you accept the idea that relationships are for healing, your dating life will immediately take on a whole new reality. You will no longer be looking for superficial things because the more you are able to accept yourself, the more you will be able to accept the truth of someone else. Meaning, the person you are dating is also wounded and needing to be healed as well, whether it's on a conscious level or not.

One of my clients recently texted me this after a first date: "I just finished a date with a guy who was never hugged by his mother."

After she slept on it, she continued the next day with: "I woke up with an icky feeling about that guy. Like a lot of emotional sludge that rubbed off on me. He was super funny, my ideal humor, really, and we kissed at the end of the night, and it was nice. But he's a comedian, and I feel like every super funny guy I've ever liked was deeply, deeply wounded and currently in a lot of pain. He had sciatica for 2 months and just recovered like 2 weeks ago. Are there any healthy ones?!?"

My response to her: "Remember, you are deeply wounded as well. No one is 'healthy.' We are all just working on ourselves. He might not be your guym but he ticks off the humor box and was honest about his childhood and pain."

I liked this guy for her, and I wanted to see how he'd continue to show up. Unfortunately, she stood by her belief that he was not right for her because he was wasn't divorced (remember, available men don't stay available for long), not working on himself (most guys aren't), was too much like her father (possibly), staying stuck in his pain (verdict was still out, he was aware of his pain and had healed his sciaticia), but I let it go until…

Women Bring the Spirituality To The Relationship

A day later my client texted me to say that she had gone out with this guy again and realized she had judged him too harshly. She was self-aware enough to know it was partially to protect herself from actually getting to know someone. She found out he was doing transcendental meditation, becoming a massage therapist, and that he thought the sciatica was the best thing that ever happened to him because it caused him to appreciate how good his life is. She felt no energetic sludge, in fact they cuddled and basically had sex all night. It was awesome for her.

Now, you might be thinking, *what, isn't she breaking all the rules?* My answer is no. This was an acceptable move for this particular client based on her wounding, which is unique to her. According to her, she felt free, open, and not attached to an outcome. This was all great, but to keep her from going down a slippery slope, I did suggest she define it for herself.

She struggled with this idea, and wanted to keep it loose, which was fine, but she still needed to define if for herself.

Setting a private intention for yourself creates a synergy and keeps things from getting messy. Think of it as internal emotional boundaries that then create external physical boundaries. A woman knows what she wants, a girl doesn't. A girl is looking to be saved, a woman isn't.

It goes back to the idea of sitting on the lotus flower: you decide what works for you and what doesn't, you communicate specific requests, not your overall view of the relationship, that's for the man, and then wait. If the man keeps showing up, and by that I mean, honors your requests, keeps asking you out, can't get enough of you, demands you to be his girlfriend —awesome, if he doesn't, move on. The man who wants to be your partner will show up and you won't have to think *is he interested*? For a man to stay in privilege in relationship the woman must stay in awe of herself, sitting on her lotus flower.

Provide, Protect, Cherish

Provide, protect, and cherish are the three desires a man has for the woman he loves. Depending on your age, this will become his role as a father as well, if you decide to have children.

This doesn't mean that you can't also provide or that you don't both provide. Think of it instead as more of an energy behind a man's intention. Is he driven to provide, protect, and cherish? If not, you might have a boy on your hands.

The key to finding out where your man stands is not to do everything for him and mother him. How you set up the relationship in the beginning is how the relationship will continue for the duration. If you ask the man out, make reservations, book romantic weekends away, pay for everything, split the bill at a restaurant, be ready for that to be your relationship.

It is very difficult to change behavior or patterns once they are established. If this is not what you want long term, then don't make it what you do in the short term.

Often, my clients ask about who should pay on dates. Money is often the cause for break-ups because money is directly influenced by morals and values. I recently dated someone who was more freed up around money, which helped me free myself up, and change my perspective, which had become more of a poverty consciousness. Unfortunately, his freedom around money also left him in debt, about to file bankruptcy. I live debt free because that is how my soul is free, so needless to say, we were not a long term match.

When we first started dating and throughout our relationship, he paid for everything, even buying me gas on occasion, which I loved because I felt safe but then it turned on its head, and I felt like it was attached to what I've come to call, *secret contracts.*

When a gift is given whether it be material goods, words, or physical touch, and there are silent strings attached, this is a secret contract. If you like your guy to pay, let him, be truthful with your feelings from the start.

If you are able to speak your truth, then you are less likely to have resentments as the relationship continues. It is not always easy to speak our truth.

Morals, Values, and a Shared Vision

If you are wondering what the secret sauce to a true love relationship is, it's having similar morals, values, and a shared vision.

I have coached several married couples and most of their fights, arguments, resentments, fall back to their very different points of view on morals and values plus they have lost sight of a shared vision. Often times they've stopped having any real communication and the relationship was set up with the woman doing more than she really wanted to do and she is now full of resentments, putting her man down all the time. The man feels small and horrible about himself. It's a horrible cycle.

A relationship exists outside of the two people, it is an entity to itself. I compare it to a garden. When two people create a garden they might have different ideas how they want their garden to look. One person might be pragmatic and only want native plants, the other person might be a dreamer and want an English garden in the desert. Can they compromise? I don't know. Dreamers are usually great at beautiful ideas but implementing and caring for the garden is a whole different story so does it then fall on the pragmatic person's to-do list to take care of the garden they didn't even want? Maybe. Can you see how just a simple question like this brings morals, values, and having a shared vision into focus?

Finding a person who shares your vision (for example, you both love roses, and both enjoy pruning and caring for the garden equally) will make for an easier relationship. If your morals and values, differ but you have a shared vision, that could work, but would be very challenging. If you are on different pages with everything, do the most healing thing for both of you and move on.

There will always be compromise, it just depends on how much you are willing and able to compromise and not feel like you are sacrificing. There needs to be a balance.

Still Interested?

Relationship isn't for everyone. Remember to be true to you. There are many ways to live your life. By going deep within, you will find what works for you. Sometimes, we have to jump into something that we have pictured as our greatest happiness to find out that it really isn't what we actually want. Then we just need to steer our ship in a different direction. Going deep within to really know who we are and offering ourselves lots of experiences is how we will discover what outer environment will free our souls completely.

There is nothing better than finding your true love, but in order to do it, being in love with yourself is essential.

Chapter 8: Let Love In

Boundaries define us. They define what is me and what is not me. A boundary shows me where I end and someone else begins, leading me to a sense of ownership.

— Henry Cloud

One of the most important attributes to living a happy life is having healthy boundaries. Unfortunately, this is a learned skill and most of our parents were not taught healthy boundaries so they were not handed down to us.

Boundaries let people know who you are. If you fall on the side of an empath, you will most likely have zero skills in setting boundaries unless you've been working on them. Boundaries will feel completely uncomfortable to you. This is because you can feel other people's pain and the thought that you created it keeps you silent. You would rather say nothing, process your own uncomfortableness and try to move on but this doesn't work and keeps you isolated and resentful.

If you fall on the tougher side with some narcissistic tendencies, then your boundaries are more like walls. Letting someone in feels incredibly vulnerable, like you will lose control or like someone will take advantage of you so you keep people out by judging them.

Not too long ago, one of my clients was dating a guy in the middle of getting his green card. A perfect storm had hit his life, and he found himself needing a place to stay for a bit. My client was so afraid she would not be able to let him in with proper boundaries and that she was about to cut him off emotionally and miss out on learning more about herself and the guy.

Fortunately, I was able to shine some perspective on it by letting her know she can set boundaries and she is not the victim of anything. She was then able to find a happy medium of having empathy and asking if he needed a place for a couple nights, knowing that through communication, even if uncomfortable she will build a deeper connection while still staying true to herself.

Without a sense of self, its incredibly difficult to do this in a healthy fashion and can become equally confusing.

Boundaries & Love

Boundaries are the foundation for a deeply connected, healthy relationship, aka, true love.

A few years ago I had a client come to the ranch to do an equine assisted coaching session with me. When she walked into the round pen, I asked her what she wanted to work on that day. She said, relationship. She mentioned that often times, she starts to date, and it seems to be going really well until something happens and she can't seem to keep the connection going.

"Got it, lets do it," I said.

I handed her four cones and asked her to create an obstacle that she would move the horse through energetically, without touching the horse. She placed the four cones in a line about one-third across the round pen and started interacting with the horse, asking the horse to move by waving her arms, and making clucking sounds. After a couple of minutes, she stepped into the quadrant of the round pen that she had marked off and when the horse tried to follow her she stopped him, keeping him out.

I couldn't believe my eyes.

She had just done exactly what she said she wanted to work on. She had created a nice connection with the horse and then put herself in a box, asking the horse to stay out.

When I asked her what she was doing, it suddenly became obvious and she burst into tears. It was a very cathartic moment. We laughed and cried.

Some of the traits of having too firm of boundaries are:

- You avoid close, intimate relationships
- You probably don't ask for help
- You might not have a lot of truly close friends
- You don't share much about yourself
- You are often detached, even when you are in a romantic relationship
- You keep your distance because you are afraid of being rejected.

If your boundaries are too lose or nonexistent, this will show up as:

- Oversharing your personal information

- Having a hard time saying 'no' to people
- Overly involved in other people's boundaries
- Receiving yourself worth from the opinions of others
- Accepting abuse or disrespect
- Acting submissively not to be rejected.

So what are healthy boundaries? They are:

- Valuing your own opinion
- Not compromising your values for others
- Sharing personal information in an appropriate way
- Knowing your wants and needs and able to communicate them
- Understanding that you can totally hear, 'no' and accept it.

A healthy person will accept your boundaries. An unhealthy person will tell you that you are wrong for having such boundaries, and will try to change your mind, judging you. Run to the hills if you meet such a person. This is most likely a maddening narcissist. If someone decides to move on because of your boundary, great, you dodged a bullet. Rejection is always protection. It's the universe having your back. Be thankful.

From reading these boundary characteristics you can probably find areas where all different boundary types play out, especially in the arena of dating, which can get very confusing because you are in the labyrinth of your own psyche, it's so easy to get lost.

Vulnerability is a Super Power

Being able to share our inner most selves is the most essential part of being a connected human. We are all born pure and open to love, but as we go through our lives, this light begins to dim due to situations that make us feel unsafe. Sometimes, we feel that we are fighting to keep ourselves safe. This survival system can create a lot of success but at some point it stops giving and begins to take.

Let's say that your childhood created an opportunity to be good, to be the best, to succeed, to be sassy, and smart, but now you feel isolated. You know there is something within you that is keeping men away and you want to break this down so that you can start a family and begin the next phase of your life.

You will need to get uncomfortable.

Changing who you are is not an easy process and is why most people do not change. Change takes a warrior's heart, but being vulnerable means you will need to have a such a heart.

If you are on lock down, you will need to learn to open up and share. If you never say, 'no' to people you will have to feel the pain of saying. 'no' and accepting the person's reaction to your 'no.' Both scenarios are equally uncomfortable and can leave one feeling that they will be attacked.

By building boundaries for ourselves, we have learned to feel safe. When we start to break down those boundaries, we often feel unsafe and vulnerable; feelings that we are taught to reject. So, instead of living in that discomfort, you build our boundaries back up, you wall yourself off in safety. I promise that no matter how much you want to believe that unhealthy boundaries allow for freedom, they won't be enough. I really wish they could be, but they won't.

I wish I could wave a magic wand over your head and give you healthy boundaries without going through feeling vulnerable, but I can't. Only you can do the work to create a new way of being in the world.

Chapter 9: Becoming the Heroine

Real love is freedom. It can stand the test of truth.

— *Eva Pierrakos*

Recently, I had a client say, "I just want to leave my childhood behind me. I'm tired of dragging it into every relationship. I want to be done." It was hard breaking the news to her that this idea is actually impossible. Our childhoods created us, they will be with us forever. There is nowhere to run except deep within, into the places that scare us, so we can shine a light on them and bring love to them. This is where the gold presides. This is where we find our self-worth, not through material belongings, beauty, or Instagram likes.

Self vs. Image

Your true self is free, spontaneous, joyous, loving, creative and giving. You are in touch with it when you are living in truth, give from your heart, and are in meditation.

Your image is created as a universal pseudo-protection from pain or wounding, which began at birth. Through your image, you try to re-establish confidence, happiness, and security by pretending to be what you are not . It was created for you to survive your neurotic family, childhood bully. You are probably not aware of this protective layer and have come to know it as you, but the truth is, it is not you. It has gotten you this far, but it is now holding you back from living fully.

How can you use your image as a super power? You need to be in relationship with it. First, you need to know that it exists and then be able to see when it is helping you or harming you. This is the essence of authenticity. Establishing a loving connection to your true self, your wounded little girl and your angry rebel, as we discussed previously.

For example, I was raised by a father who offered me love only when I did something to please him, otherwise I wasn't good enough. He didn't just love me for me, so I was always trying to prove that I was worthy of love by being capable, smart, and responsible. I've grown to call this need to prove I'm lovable and worthy the "monkey dance."

I became a woman who could handle anything. I am tough, a know-it-all, competent, controlled, and unexpressed. Yes, all of these attributes of my image kept me alive, but they also cut me off from deep connection to people and definitely kept me out of relationship.

Why did I create this image? To receive love and not be abandoned. I figured that if I showed up a certain way, the way my father approved of, then I'd be loved and I wouldn't be left.

When you are able to accept the rougher edges of yourself, that part of you that doesn't believe you are worthy, something really beautiful happens. You are able to accept yourself for who you are, which is powerful because when the mask begins to dissolve, the image begins to integrate. Once you are able to accept who you are, you are also able to accept others for who they are, which allows you to see reality without projections, connect more deeply and be in authentic relationships with people and the world.

The truth is that we are all wounded. We all feel unloveable, unworthy, abandoned, and not good enough. We all try to make ourselves feel better through sex, drugs, prescription drugs, material things, career success, relationship, but the truth is the only way to feel love, worthy, good enough, and to never feel abandoned is to love our selves —to go deep into those dark places that we've been avoiding and know that we are ok.

When I was 25, I *fell in love* with a pot-growing, alcoholic. He was a bad boy with a capitol B. This guy was everything I thought I wasn't — free, charismatic, gorgeous, and powerful. The freedom is what I really desired. It felt like nothing affected him, which was the opposite of my own emotional state. Before meeting him, I had been a career driven young woman about to move to LA to further myself as a filmmaker, but after meeting him I decided to stay in Seattle and help him with his feature film.

However, as the relationship progressed, I became a shadow of my former self. This guy didn't love me, nor was he capable of love. I did everything to try and get him to love me, just like I did with my father. I became a shadow of my former self. I had lost touch with my true self, and truly believed I could not survive without him. I was fully in my image. Some people call this love but it's actually raging co-dependence. Looking back, it's clear that he was a narcissist, and I was a depressed empath.

It's not hard to believe what happened next — he cheated on me. I hit my lowest point, wanting to die. After he broke my heart, one fateful morning, I had a vision. It wasn't something that happened every day (or ever), which is why I remember it so clearly. I was half awake, half asleep, when I felt a warm, kind and loving energy enfold me. It was the most love I had ever felt. It felt like I, or an aspect of myself, the best part of me, was full of love. The vision showed me that I could love myself, but not only that, but that it was necessary. I was all I needed, and the rest was whatever I made it.

This was my first experience of God or Spirit. It was after this vision that I became a true seeker.

Escaping the Heath

Why is this so important to relationship? When you are in relationship, your stuff gets turned upside down and inside out, whether you want it to or not. How many times have you heard, "I'm not dating, I'm just going to work on myself?" This is impossible.

When I was single, I had my stuff handled. Everything was buttoned up tight. I thought I was healthy and strong. I thought that when I found relationship, it would unfold easily before me because of all the work I had done. It was pure fantasy. As soon as I was in relationship, all of the stuff I thought had been healed began to rise to the surface again.

For example, when I first moved into the house with my partner and our children, my control issues went on over-drive. When my partner took my NutriBullet container to work, I found myself nearly having a panic attack. I thought to myself, *what the fuck? This is out of control.*

When I lived alone with just my son, everything was under my control and all was good. Having someone else in the house, using my stuff, was truly triggering. Luckily, I was able to see it, take a deep breath, unpack the fear, have compassion for myself then let it go. It is only in relationship that we can heal or up-level.

I like to think of life as a video game. Your life is the result of the choices you've made. You've been co-creating your life from the day you were born, consciously or unconsciously. I realize that his can be tricky to hear, but it can also be freeing to move forward.

Let's play with an idea for a minute … Suspend your disbelief, and imagine that before landing on earth, you signed a sacred contract, where you chose everything, all the lessons your life has given you up until this point. Imagine that you are the victim of nothing and every lesson is for you to have an experience to heal? How does that feel?

I recently had a client go to Boston because I man she'd had a couple flings with wanted her to go out. He hadn't said, "Come out and stay with me," or anything. It was more like, "Come out, and we'll get together." Once she got there and reached out, he didn't make a plan with her, nor did he make any attempt to see her. So she left without seeing him. This was incredibly painful for her and she had a good cry.

She will continue to receive this lesson until she decides she is worthy of someone's affection and love or gets deeply in touch with her no current, which is still in the shadows. Going to Boston was the best thing she could have done because it became clear he was not truly interested, and she was able to pop the fantasy bubble and move on once and for all.

Once we surrender to the idea that everything is happening for our greatest good, we choose to wake up and not be the victim. This is awakening. When you are fully awake, you walk into situation, eyes wide open, feelers out, like a heroine ready to discover friends, foes, mentors, oracles, tricksters, fools, allies, and lovers. You might choose to put yourself in situations that are challenging and expansive. When you are willing to go into the labyrinth of your soul, all of life becomes a grand mystery.

With a lot of self-work, the world becomes a place to receive information, so what you see on the outside is what's going on, on the inside. With enough practice, we are able to read the signs for the next direction we are meant to go, if we allow. It's the practice of surrender, a completely letting go.

Imagine yourself as a leaf floating down the creek. Trust that if we do not brace or tense, we will gracefully, float around the rocks, trusting the speed of the water, knowing that we are safe, even if we get caught on a rock for a while. Trust and knowing are everything.

Then life becomes a never-ending video game with limitless levels. You will complete a level and move on to the next. However, if you refuse to wake up, you repeat the same lesson over and over and that's when people become depressed. A relationship can become a prison, but because we feel safe in it, we don't venture out. The truth can be said for being single. It feels safe, so we find ways to sabotage ourselves blaming the lack of good men, or the world for the fact that we are single. Are we brave enough to say, *hell yeah!*

Chapter 10: Fairy Dust and a Little Magic

The world is full of magic things, patiently waiting for our senses to grow sharper.

— W.B. Yeats

Let's take a collective sigh. We've come so far. Now, its time to have a little fun. Let's go back to the romance we started this journey with, before we covered the wounding and the boundaries where things got a little serious and we forgot the magic required for falling in love, as Frank Sinatra says, "Because I love you, just the way you look tonight." We imagine him singing to a Grace Kelly type character in an elegant black dress, gorgeous, but who knows, maybe he was singing to someone who just had a baby, sweaty and a mess, or a woman working through her own wounding, vulnerable and scared wearing sweats, hair pulled up, tear streaked face.

The point is, be who you are. Share with your man, once you have him, all your ugly. It is the only way to know if he really loves you or if he is in some sort of fantasy or maybe it's your fantasy?

We are always growing. In every partnership. You are either growing, transforming or dying on the vine. I believe we have all witnessed or experienced the dying on the vine experience. Let's create a love life that resembles what we see in the movies, right? The romance of the greatest love songs? To do this, we need a little magic, along with everything we have covered: wounding, heartbreak, vulnerability. openness, kindness, and always a solid look at ourselves in truth.

Because if you think you can keep perfection, be guarded, in fear and fall in love, you are mistaken. The glory of love is in the trenches. You will discover this once you find your love, if and when you choose to have children. I learned this with my son Cole. He prepared me for what true love is, and it's nothing like the fantasy of love. It's a wild ride.

So let's get to the magic.

Two years ago, while shopping in Trader Joe's, I received an unusual phone call from a client and her fiancé. As I rolled my cart aimlessly around the store, they asked me to officiate their wedding in New Orleans on New Year's Eve. I was flabbergasted, taken aback, in awe. I had been asking Spirit to make my life bigger. I was so honored to officiate their wedding. I loved them both so much. Something was shifting.

Fast forward a couple months to New Orleans, New Year's Eve, 2016, I'm standing in front of about 75 people in a gorgeous Garden District mansion, asking everyone to take a deep breath to become present to the ceremony but I was unable to take one myself, choking on my own nerves. I was terrified. I struggled to get the second breath choked down, when suddenly the vent came on and air shot up my back, blowing my hair and dress up! 'Thank you Spirit!' From that moment on, I was able to relax and continue to do the ceremony with levity. It was so beautiful and a great success.

Something began to shift inside me and I could feel deep down that I was finally ready to be in partnership. There was something about officiating, creating the ceremony, being a part of their family, friends, relatives that had me wanting to create a vision with someone and share my life. After 46 years, I was ready to be in relationship. I was ready to face the music that I had been avoiding in false serenity.

This is where I began to bring in the magic.

Talismans

My first talisman was created on this wedding night. For years I had slept with two 30mm Feng Shui quartz crystal tear drops that hung on my bed post, but they had lost power, having been through the mourning of Ken, lost lovers, and some of my belief. They just hung there, collecting dust. I'd brush them off ever-so-often and do my best to imbue them with some sort of intention, but it was a lame attempt. I bet you know what I'm talking about, you read somewhere that by doing one thing or another, it helps you draw in your true love, but you are still somehow alone?

Yeah, that's what those two crystals hanging on my bedpost collecting dust were to me: forgotten dreams. I really didn't believe I deserved or would ever receive true love. But something shifted the night of the wedding.

That night, we all received vintage handkerchiefs for The Second Line of the wedding. The night was ridiculously crazy, with us cutting the bottom of the bride's dress off around 2am in a bar. At 5am, four of us, including the bride, found ourselves enjoying warm beignets and coffee at Café Du Monde. Somehow, I had managed to hang on to my handkerchief all night. I don't know how. When I got back to Los Angeles after the wedding, I kissed the handkerchief, which was white with a read embroidered edge and a red heart, and I put it under my pillow. I believed this handkerchief would bring me love. I even dusted off my twin crystals one more time, with deep intention that it was happening. It was time.

God Damn Vision Boards!

Argh, I never imagined myself writing about vision boards, and yet, here I am. I spent a large portion of my professional life hating vision boards. They seemed like a stupid *Law of Attraction* trick. If done right, from a place of love and co-creation, vision boards can help pin point a vision and help it become real.

During the same year of the wedding, I made two vision boards. It started when a new client made a vision board and wanted me to intuitively interpret her board. It was so powerful and beautiful. She had chosen some amazing and intuitive images. It was a piece of art and was the landscape of her soul that I could read like a palm reader.

I decided there was something to this vision board thing and that it was slightly brilliant. I had my two women's groups create vision boards, and I did it with them. After creating them, I stuck them up in my closet, where I could see them but have to pay daily attention to them if I didn't want to.

As you can see in the two vision boards, I didn't have a picture of a wedding or a man per say, but I did have how I wanted to be in the world and how I wanted to be received. I wanted to alter my boundaries, be loving, trust, have no agenda, and go beyond my own limiting beliefs. In the board on the right, I wanted to bring in more of my femininity and have someone see me as unexpected brilliance. You see, it's not about finding the right image to reflect your fantasy. I was able to manifest my next lover by intuitively building a tapestry of love around me. By creating a reflection of my own brilliance, I was letting myself be vulnerable, letting the world know how to embrace me.

Unfortunately, the biggest mistake people make when they are creating vision boards is creating them from their heads. Its incredibly difficult to create anything from only the head because its uninspired. Often times, when I'm working with people and horses, I see people struggle to try and create something from their head. They think they can make the horse move by thinking. It will never happen. You have to move the horse from the heart, head, and gut! That is where the power exists to create anything. This is the mana of life. Art, life, everything is created through the power of focused intention and channeling your energy towards the intention without being attached to an outcome.

Out With The Old

In 2007, I was engaged to be married. Our 'meet cute' was at a café. I was meeting with producers that day about a script I'd written, but I couldn't focus once the guy walked in. He sat outside facing me, and we flirted with our eyes.

Walking back to my car, I saw him again, from the corner of my eye, driving toward me. He stopped right in front of me and hollered out, 'Do you want to go dancing?'

"Yes," I yelled back as I ran up to his van.

Within six weeks, we were engaged and had planned a wedding in Vegas for the next month. I bought a beautiful wedding dress that had a princess feel to it, a full tulle skirt lined with pink satin and an embroidered corseted halter top. I was in pure fantasy. I thought I had met my prince charming and I wanted to be his princess.

Needless to say, we never got married. We were not a fit, nor were we healthy enough to create a healthy relationship from our differences. Soon after we broke up, I was told by a psychic friend that I needed to get rid of the dress. For whatever reason, this proved to be incredibly difficult. I gave it to a friend, to see if she wanted it for her wedding, and she had it for several months before returning it. Then I had a friend model it and try to sell it for me for 20% of the sale. I even tried to give it away when a wedding shop folded and there were a bunch of brides that weren't getting their dresses, but no one would take it. I finally resorted to taking it and all its accessories to Goodwill.

Giving the dress away pulled at all my heart strings. It wasn't easy to do, but it was necessary to my own emotional cleansing. By throwing out the old, you are able to create a space that allows for magic to flourish.

Intention Setting

Remember the journal writing I shared in Chapter 4? This can be an awesome exercise. All you need to do is find a quiet place to sit for about twenty minutes, take a few deep breaths until you feel you are centered, and your attention is in your lower heart chakra, then from that place write how you want your life to be in the future but write it as if it's the present moment. Include how you spend your time, how you want your man to love you and acknowledge you. Also, include how you will love your man, share your life with him, and show him your love.

Done correctly, this can be pretty powerful stuff.

Faith and Knowing

Whether you are religious or not, it doesn't matter. Remember you are special, but not so special that you are going to end up the crazy cat lady dying alone. If you are reading this book, your energetic signature doesn't have crazy cat lady in it.

You must know that your man is walking towards you and he is equally excited to meet you. All the negative thoughts, about how there aren't enough men, they all want someone that isn't you, you aren't pretty enough, smart enough needs to stop. Replace such negative thinking with positive thoughts. Know he is coming towards you and you are worthy. It only takes one man so make the path to finding him an adventure. If you are negative along the path, you will most likely be negativity into the relationship. How you do one thing is how you do everything.

We create our lives through our thoughts. Why not create something really beautiful? It's totally up to you. You are co-creating your life! Make it beautiful.

Chapter 11: Barriers and Checkpoints

It is precisely because we resist the darkness in ourselves that we miss the depths of the loveliness, beauty, brilliance, creativity, and joy that lie at our core.

— *Thomas Moore*

We have come far on this journey and you've been given a lot of information and tips on how to find love without settling. And yet, if it were as easy as reading a book, you would have already found your true love. I'm sure this is not the first or only book you have read on this topic. I know I've read at least 20 books on how to find love. The truth is that finding true love is a much more complicated process than finding someone you are happy enough to settle down with. True love is for the brave, the warrior hearted, the poets, the patient, the wild ones.

Every word written in this book is a beacon for you to follow. But the road can be long and it is easy to lose site of the light and go off into the woods. Sometimes we can find a beautiful lesson lost in the woods but other times we are just rambling around, afraid, and soon we need to rest. What might make you lose sight and have you lost in the woods?

Change is incredibly uncomfortable. This is the number one reason why people don't do it. Often times the universe pushes us into lessons to see if we will wake up, or in other words change the course of our lives. Being loved can feel incredibly uncomfortable especially if it is new to us. We do not grow without getting uncomfortable.

Whenever I start working with a new client, I get excited for them because I know they are ready and committed to taking the first real step on the path to change their life. They no longer want to day dream but to live their dream. It's a big deal. I also know that you can't do this alone. Whether it's a therapist, coach, a friend, or someone to keep you accountable, everyone needs someone to help through the transition of leveling up.

We don't know where the new path is going to take us and this alone could keep us from taking a our first step. There are many reasons why you've been single, but I'll guess the number one reason you've remained single is because, in some way, its comfortable. I get it. The beginning of any new adventure is exciting, but at some point, we'll want to quit. It's totally normal.

Doubts

When you are dating, doubt will creep in. Its inevitable. You will doubt that there are any good men left. You will doubt if you really want a relationship, saying things like, *I'm just not meant to be in relationship. Honestly, I'm happy on my own.* This doubt will create all sorts of negative stories in your brain that you will then believe.

I recently had a client full of doubt about on-line dating. She had switched her profile to a different service but was really wanting to take a break from it, as she focused more on meeting guys in person. I suggested she not take a total break from on-line dating but perhaps not put so much focus on it. That was a couple weeks ago, she just texted me that she's been on a second date with a single dad that she really liked and was excited about. She met him online.

Self-Sabotage

Out of all the obstacles that can come up on your search for love, this might be the trickiest because we really can't see the back of our heads. Can you imagine trying to cut your own hair in the back? It would be a disaster. Self-sabotage is really hard to see, almost impossible without another set of eyes.

I have a client I've been working with for years on many different areas of her life. In the background, she's always had a desire for a relationship, but it was never her focus until recently. A few months ago, she said she was finally ready to be in a relationship. So, we began to set an intention and work on it, but then she continued to travel, a lot. I finally told her that if she really wanted a relationship, she was going to have to stay put, no travel for at least three months.

She didn't see the travel as a way of sabotaging her dating but it was. To most, including her, travel looked exciting and fun, like making the most out of being single, but in actuality she was running from herself and her fear of failure.

Confusion

As we begin to peel back the layers to our true selves and learn how to be more feminine, set proper boundaries, and sit on our lotus flowers, it can become very confusing. These are new tools. You are creating a new way of being in the world and it is easy to get lost. I'm not sure how anyone could do this on their own. Confusion can show up in many areas, to stay with a guy or not stay? Am I mothering? Am I settling? Is it me or him?

I was asked by a client not too long ago what is the difference between nurturing and mothering? She wanted to be generous, kind, and caring while still holding her boundaries and not mothering the guy she was dating. She asked if it was possible to be nurturing with a man?

My response to her is that yes, it is possible to be nurturing to a man. You nurture a man to follow his dreams, his hobbies, get a different job, start a new career path by cherishing an ambition for him. Mothering is telling him how to do it. Did you send your resume out today? You need to look on-line to see if they are hiring. Did you fill out your application?

Asking such questions is belittling and emasculating. I gave her specific examples of how she could honor and support the guy without being mothering.

All of this can become very confusing as we shed old patterns that feel very real to us.

Conclusion

Just when the caterpillar thought the world was over it became a butterfly.

— *English Proverb*

When I started writing this book, my dream was for you to find love without settling, that it can be fun and perhaps discover what it is that keeps you from finding it. Love is a tricky thing. It is not to be controlled and there is no one way to find and hold onto it but hopefully now you are more able to appreciate the journey and release your grasp on the destination.

With that being said, life is a grand adventure and the best part of life is all the experiences we open ourselves up to. =My wish for you is to have your dreams fulfilled, to meet a man that you love truly, madly, deeply and to start a family.

Perhaps now you feel that by going a little deeper into your self and allowing your self to have experiences without being too attached to the outcome that you are creating a synergy to attract the one.

Maybe you have a new found enthusiasm for dating and are feeling more empowered with your knowledge of staying out of fantasy, keeping tabs on the denial, and living fully in reality.

Remember, you are a strong feminine energy and keeping your connection to self is worth more than any relationship. This will make you a good mama as well and an unforgettable partner and woman. It's also a skill you will want to teach your little ones.

Your little girl and your inner rebel can be your best friends, they no longer need to stay buried or abandoned. Parent them, and they will not run the show. Rather, they will play an active part in your quest for love, helping you to become a fully realized mature woman.

Relationships can be tricky and setting them up without resentment even trickier, but if we acknowledge that relationships are for healing, we are more able to have compassion for ourselves and our partners.

Boundaries are the key to a healthy relationship and speaking your truth is the secret sauce. Both might be new tools but if you are able to practice them and implement them while dating, your chances of having a successful relationship are greater.

Maybe you've never thought about the possibility that we are all wounded souls, or maybe you wanted to leave your childhood behind. But now you see that owning you're wounding and seeing your dates and potential partners with their wounding will illuminate greater possibility for a deeper connection.

Don't ever forget that you are an amazing woman worthy of love. When you hear stories in you head that tell you otherwise, replace them with my voice, telling you that life is a miraculous journey and as long you enjoy the experiences, even some of the tougher ones, you can't go wrong. If you love the journey, the destination matters less.

Thank You

Thanks for reading! I'd love to hear more about you, your dating, what has you stuck? All the good stuff. Please email me at stacey@staceyjwarner.com

FREE INTENTION SETTING CRYSTAL

Let me help you get started with setting your intention for finding true love but sending you a blessed 30mm Feng Shui crystal. Here's what you need to do to get it:

1. Schedule a strategy session with me by emailing me at stacey@staceyjwarner.com.
2. Show up for the scheduled strategy session. Showing up is where the magic begins. Perhaps the first step for making your life what you want it.
3. During the session, please mention the crystal to me so I can give it a unique blessing just for you before sending it.

Once you receive your crystal, be sure to share it and tag me on Facebook or Instagram.

About The Author

Stacey J. Warner is a Certified Life Coach, Equus Coach, and Yoga Teacher. A seeker her entire life, she walks the walk. In 2011, as a single mother, age 41, she left a comfortable, reliable film industry job in Los Angeles, moved to Austin, TX and became a Certified Life Coach. Frightening as it was, "I'm so glad I had the guts to do it. The challenges of being an entrepreneur forced me to grow and expand in ways I didn't think were possible."

Her life continues to expand after creating and facilitating her own programs on breaking up subconscious patterns.She truly believes everyone deserves finding true love and has dedicated her business to helping successful women do just that. She understands first hand the many choices women must make regarding their careers, starting a family, and finding love without settling.

Her exclusive one-on-one retreats are curated for the individual's soul down to the location, and could include yoga, equine assisted coaching, walks on the beach, hikes in the redwoods, or wine tasting. She is an author, write, filmmaker, and has trained with leading professionals in all her fields. She received her BA in Drama from the University of Washington.

www.staceyjwarner.com
stacey@staceyjwarner.com